The Ultimate Halogen

Oven Recipe Book

Discover Delicious and Easy Recipes That You Can Make
in Your Halogen Oven!

BY: Allie Allen

COOK & ENJOY

Copyright 2020 Allie Allen

Copyright Notes

My Gift to You for Buying My Book!

I would like to extend an exclusive offer to receive free and discounted eBooks every day! This special gift is my way of saying thanks. If you fill in the subscription box below you will begin to receive special offers directly to your email.

Not only that! You will also receive notifications letting you know when an offer will expire. You will never miss a chance to get a free book! Who wouldn't want that?

Fill in the subscriber information below and get started today!

https://allie-allen.getresponsepages.com/

Table of Contents

Introduction

Have you purchased a Halogen oven but aren't sure where to begin? Or are you looking for delicious new recipes that you can make in your Halogen oven? If so, then this recipe book is for you! Filled with 30 delicious recipes, there's something that everyone is sure to love in here!

From delicious appetizers to mains and even a few desserts, you can cook up all sorts of deliciousness in your oven with the help of this book. Plus, all of the recipes are detailed and come with step-by-step instructions, making it perfect for even the most beginner cook! So, what are you waiting for? Let's begin!

Lemony Roast Turkey

Delicious and moist lemony roast turkey with thyme.

Makes: 2 servings

Prep: 10 min

Cook: 45 min

Ingredients:

- 10 pounds turkey crown
- 1 lemon, halved
- 2 tablespoons olive oil
- 1 bulb garlic, halved
- Salt and freshly ground pepper to taste
- 2 bay leaves
- 1 bunch thyme

Directions:

To prepare the turkey, cut off excess fat and giblets. Wash and pat dry. Brush the turkey with olive oil, and salt and freshly ground black pepper. Put bay leaves, lemon, garlic, and thyme into the cavity of the turkey.

Turn the temperature of your halogen oven at 430F. Place the turkey on the low wire rack. Let it cook for 1 hour. Reduce temperature to 350F. Turn the turkey over and cook for another 45 minutes or until well cooked.

Serve.

Easy Halogen Chicken

A delicious and easy chicken recipe with garlic and parsnips.

Makes: 4 servings

Prep: 10 min

Cook: 40 min

Ingredients:

- 1.5kg chicken, wash, pat dry
- 4 garlic cloves
- 2 medium carrots
- 2 white onions
- 2 medium parsnips
- 2 tablespoons cooking oil
- 2 cups chicken broth
- 2 tablespoons white flour
- Salt and pepper, to taste

Directions:

Preheat your oven to 400F for 3 minutes.

Arrange garlic, carrots, parsnips and onions on the low rack of your halogen oven. Rub chicken with oil, salt, and pepper, and put on the low rack on top of the vegetables. Cook for 35 minutes. If chicken isn't done, cook for another 5 minutes or until well cooked.

Remove from the oven and keep warm. Pour cooking liquid in a saucepan, add flour, and mix well. Stir in chicken broth and cook to thicken. Top each serving of chicken with gravy.

Rosemary Stuffed Chicken

Delicious rosemary stuffed chicken recipe with sun-dried tomatoes.

Makes: 4 servings

Prep: 10 min

Cook: 30 min

Ingredients:

- 4 chicken breasts, skinless
- ¼ cup sun-dried tomatoes, chopped
- 4 prosciutto ham slices
- 1 tablespoon rosemary, fresh, chopped
- 4 tablespoons ricotta cheese
- 1 teaspoon thyme, fresh, chopped

Directions:

Before you begin cooking, heat your oven at 375F. Gently make small pockets on each chicken breast. Set aside. In a bowl, combine rosemary, cheese, tomatoes, and thyme. Mix well. Fill the pockets on the chicken breast with equal proportions of rosemary mixture. Enfold each chicken breast with a slice of ham and arrange in a roasting dish. Put on the low rack of your preheated oven and roast for about 30 minutes or until the meat is well cooked.

Serve.

Cheesy Chicken

A delicious and easy chicken recipe with just 3 ingredients!

Makes: 4 servings

Prep: 5 min

Cook: 40 min

Ingredients:

- 4 chicken breasts, skinless
- ¼ cup parmesan cheese, grated
- 4 tablespoons mayo

Directions:

Preheat your oven to 480F.

In an oven safe dish, add chicken breasts. Brush with mayonnaise and top with cheese. Carefully put the dish on the bottom rack of your halogen oven. Cook for 40 min/until juices run clear.

Herbed Turkey

A delicious turkey recipe with flavorful herbs.

Makes: 2 servings

Prep: 10 min

Cook: 1 hr.

Ingredients:

- 4 lb. turkey joint, skinless, boneless
- 1 handful chopped thyme
- Juice and zest from 1 lemon
- 1 garlic clove, chopped finely
- 1 handful parsley, chopped
- 1 red pepper, chopped finely
- Salt & ground black pepper to taste
- ¼ cup chicken stock
- ½ cup apricots, dried, chopped
- 1 chopped celery stick
- ½ cup olive oil
- 2 cups breadcrumbs, fresh
- 6 rashers streaky bacon
- 1 onion, chopped finely

Directions:

When ready to cook, heat your oven at 410F. Add half of the olive oil in a skillet and heat over medium. When hot, add onion, garlic, red pepper, and celery. Cook until vegetables are tender, about 6 to 10 minutes. Mix in lemon juice and zest, breadcrumbs, apricots, parsley, and thyme. Season to taste.

Mix in chicken stock, remove from heat. Stuff the turkey using apricot mixture, secure so that the stuffing remains intact. Rub with reserved olive oil and wrap with bacon. Enfold with foil and put on the low rack of the preheated oven. Let it roast for about 30 minutes for every kilo of meat and an additional 30 minutes. During the final 30 min, remove the foil. Ensure the turkey gets well cooked.

Roast Chicken and Potatoes

Cook an entire chicken in your halogen oven with this recipe!

Makes: 4 servings

Prep: 10 min

Cook: 35 min

Ingredients:

- 1 small whole chicken, wash, pat dry
- 4 potatoes, peeled, diced
- Cooking oil

Directions:

Add potatoes in a saucepan and cover with lightly salted water. Cook until lightly softened. Remove from heat and drain. Set aside.

Attach the extender ring on your oven. Heat oven to 375F. Put chicken on the high rack and boiled potatoes on the bottom rack. Drizzle potatoes with little oil.

Cook chicken and potatoes for 35 min. Flip your chicken over & cook for another 35 minutes or until juices run clear and potatoes are crispy.

Halogen Chicken in Bacon

Chicken with bacon, barbeque sauce and parmesan.

Makes: 4 servings

Prep: 5 min

Cook: 30 min

Ingredients:

- 4 smoked bacon rashers
- 4 chicken breast fillets
- BBQ sauce, to taste
- Grated parmesan cheese, to taste
- Salt and pepper, to taste

Directions:

Season chicken with salt and pepper. Brush with BBQ sauce and drizzle with parmesan cheese. Fold bacon rashers around chicken breast. Place on the bottom rack and cook for 30 minutes at 390F. Turn chicken once during cooking so that all sides get cooked.

Japanese Chicken Wings

Delicious and moist Japanese chicken wings recipe.

Makes: 4 servings

Prep: 3 hrs.

Cook: 20 min

Ingredients:

- 1 pound chicken wings, excess fat trimmed off
- 1 tablespoon ginger, finely chopped
- 2 tablespoons apple cider vinegar
- 2 tablespoons vinegar
- ½ cup soy sauce
- 1 garlic clove, crushed

Directions:

In a bowl, add garlic, ginger, sherry, and soy sauce. Place chicken wings in a large bowl. Add garlic mixture, gently toss to coat wings with the mixture. Put to marinade covered for 3 hours.

Remove wings from marinade and put on the high rack. Cook for 10 minutes at 350F. Turn chicken wings over &cook for another 10 minutes or until juices run clear.

Honey Roast Chicken

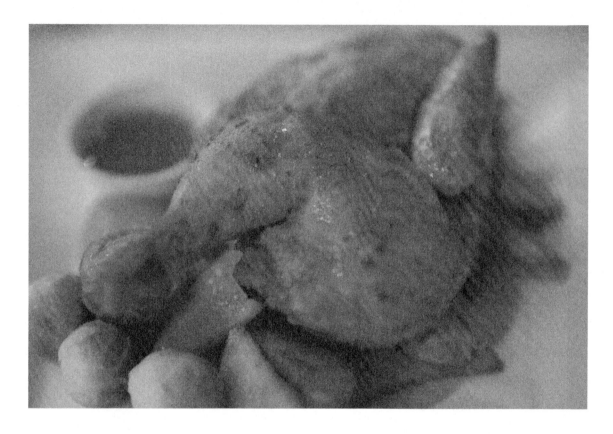

Honey roasted chicken with pecans and Dijon mustard.

Makes: 4 servings

Prep: 15 min

Cook: 15 min

Ingredients:

- ¼ cup honey
- 1 pound chicken tenderloin
- ½ cup pecans, chopped
- ½ teaspoon paprika
- 2 tablespoons Dijon mustard
- ¼ teaspoon garlic powder
- ¼ teaspoon black pepper
- 1 ¼ cups corn flake crumbs
- ½ teaspoon salt
- Cooking spray

Directions:

In a bowl, add mustard, garlic powder, paprika, and honey. Set aside. Season chicken with salt & pepper, & place in a sealable plastic bag. Add honey mixture, toss to coat well.

In a separate bowl, add pecans and corn flakes. Toss chicken in the mixture and place in an oven safe dish. Place on the bottom rack and cook for 7 minutes at 400F. Flip chicken over and cook for another 7 minutes or until done.

Mushroom and Beef

Delicious mushroom and beef recipe with onions and carrots.

Makes: 4 servings

Prep: 10 min

Cook: 1 hr. 45 min

Ingredients:

- 12 button mushrooms
- 1.5 lb. stewing beef, cut into bite size pieces
- 1 cup beef stock
- 1 tablespoon olive oil
- Salt & ground black pepper to taste
- 2 tablespoon flour
- 1 large onion, finely chopped
- 2 large carrots, sliced

Directions:

Preheat your oven to 375F. Heat olive in a skillet over medium heat. Coat meat with flour and cook in hot oil for 2 minutes. Remove from heat & place in a casserole dish. Add mushrooms, carrots, and onions. Sprinkle with red wine and beef stock. Season to taste with salt and pepper. Put the casserole on the low rack and let it cook for 1 hour and 45 min/until the meat is well cooked.

Halogen Cheese Cake

Serve up cheesecake in your halogen oven with this easy recipe!

Makes: 8 servings

Prep: 10 min

Cook: 20 min

Ingredients:

- 2 (8 ounces each) cream cheese, low fat, room temperature
- 1 cup coconut
- ½ cup brown sugar
- Sugar free caramel ice cream topping
- 2 eggs
- ¼ cup butter
- 1 teaspoon vanilla
- ½ cup pecans, chopped
- 1 graham cracker crust, low-fat
- Little chocolate covered caramel candies

Directions:

Combine pecans, butter, and coconut in cake pan (8''). Place the pan on the high rack of your oven. Set temperature at 400F. Cook for 4 minutes. Stir occasionally to prevent coconut from burning.

Mix eggs, vanilla, cream cheese, and sugar in a food processor and process until well blended. Spoon half of egg mixture into graham crackers. Add half of coconut mixture. Sprinkle with ice cream topping. Cover with reserved egg mixture.

Place on the low rack of your oven, set temperature at 325F and bake for 20 minutes. Add reserved coconut mixture. Sprinkle with topping. Garnish with chocolate covered candies. Chill in the refrigerator before serving.

Halogen Baked Pineapple

This baked pineapple recipe is a quick and easy dessert option!

Makes: 6 servings

Prep: 10 min

Cook: 40 min

Ingredients:

- 2 (20 ounces each) cans pineapple, crushed, drained
- 2 eggs
- 1 teaspoon ground cinnamon
- ¼ cup water
- 2 tablespoons corn flour
- 1 cup sugar
- 1 tablespoon butter
- 1 tablespoon vanilla

Directions:

Prepare a casserole dish by lightly coating with cooking spray. Set aside. Combine water, eggs, corn flour, sugar, and vanilla. Stir to mix well. Mix in pineapple. Transfer pineapple mixture into the prepared casserole. Add cinnamon and butter. Place on the low rack of your oven and bake for 38 minutes at 375F.

Halogen Roasted Potatoes

A delicious roasted potatoes recipe.

Makes: 2 servings

Prep: 5 min

Cook: 15 min

Ingredients:

- 2 sweet potatoes, peeled, cubed
- 1 pinch ground cloves
- 1 teaspoon cinnamon
- 2 tablespoons olive oil
- ½ teaspoon cayenne
- ¼ cup brown sugar
- ½ teaspoon salt

Directions:

In a large roasting dish, add potatoes, cinnamon, cayenne, cloves, salt, and olive oil. Mix well. Put the roasting dish on the high rack of your oven and roast for 15 minutes at 450F. Stir often. Ensure the potatoes get tender.

Gingery Beef

Asian inspired ginger beef recipe.

Makes: 8 servings

Prep: 10 min

Cook: 1 hr. 10 min

Ingredients:

- 20 ounces lean braising steak, cut into bite-size cubes
- 3 cm ginger, fresh, grated
- ½ bunch spring onions
- 2 celery sticks
- ½ teaspoon red chili, dried
- 2 tablespoons water
- 2 Red peppers, cored, chopped
- 1 tablespoon corn flour
- 1 tablespoon dark soy sauce
- 3 tablespoons oil
- 14 fluidounces beef stock
- 7 ounces sugar snap peas, halved

Directions:

In a frying pan, add 2 tbsp. of oil and heat over medium-high. Add beef and cook until browned. Place browned meat into a casserole dish or any other oven safe dish. Set aside.

In the same frying pan, add reserved cooking oil and heat over medium. Cook red pepper and celery until tender. Add celery and pepper to browned beef. Sprinkle with chili. Add soy sauce and ginger. Put on the bottom rack and cook for 50 minutes at 400F. Ensure sure it's tender and well cooked. Mix in spring onions and snap peas.

In a small bowl, combine corn flour and water, and pour over beef. Mix well and cook for 10 minutes.

Honey Roast Chicken

Roasted chicken with walnuts and honey.

Makes: 4 servings

Prep: 15 min

Cook: 15 min

Ingredients:

- ¼ cup honey
- 1 pound chicken tenderloin
- ½ cup walnuts, chopped
- ½ teaspoon paprika
- 2 tablespoons Dijon mustard
- ½ teaspoon salt
- ¼ teaspoon garlic powder
- ¼ teaspoon black pepper
- 1 ¼ cups corn flake crumbs
- Cooking spray

Directions:

In a bowl, add mustard, garlic powder, paprika, and honey. Set aside. Season chicken with salt and pepper, and place in a sealable plastic bag. Add honey mixture, toss to coat well.

In a separate bowl, add pecans and corn flakes. Toss chicken in the mixture and place in an oven safe dish. Place on the bottom rack and cook for 7 minutes at 400F. Flip chicken over & cook for another 7 minutes or until done.

Roasted Veggies

Easy roasted veggie recipe that can be used with just about any veggies!

Makes: 2 servings

Prep: 10 min

Cook: 45 min

Ingredients:

- 12 cherry tomatoes
- 2 white onions, quartered
- 4 small new potatoes, scrubbed
- 1 orange pepper, seeds removed, thinly sliced
- 1 red pepper, thinly sliced, seeds removed
- 10 garlic cloves
- 2 tablespoons olive oil
- 1 courgetti, sliced
- 1 green pepper, seeds removed, thinly sliced
- Salt and pepper to taste
- 1 teaspoon mixed herbs
- 3 large quartered chestnut mushrooms

Directions:

In a large roasting dish or pan, add potatoes, mushrooms, garlic cloves, onions, pepper, mixed herbs, courgetti, and cherry tomatoes. Sprinkle with salt & pepper. Drizzle with olive oil & place on the lower rack of your oven. Set temperature at 375F and roast for 35 minutes.

Garlic Prawn

Roasted prawns with garlic and lemon juice.

Makes: 4 servings

Prep: 5 min

Cook: 10 min

Ingredients:

- 1.5 lb. prawns, peeled
- 1 garlic clove, minced
- 2 teaspoons lemon juice, fresh
- ¼ cup margarine

Directions:

Preheat your oven to 420F.

In a small bowl, add garlic, margarine, and lemon juice. Mix to blend. Brush prawns with garlic mix. Put on the top rack of your oven. Grill prawns for 10 minutes, turning once during grilling.

Halogen Lamb Chops

Delicious lamb chops with mint and lemon juice.

Makes: 2 servings

Prep: 5 min

Cook: 10 min

Ingredients:

- 2 lamb chops
- 2 tablespoons mint, fresh
- Salt & freshly ground black pepper, to taste
- Freshly squeezed juice from half a lemon
- 2 tablespoons marmalade

Directions:

Preheat your oven to 420F.

Sprinkle lamb chops with salt & pepper and put on the high rack of your oven. Cook for 10 minutes, turning once during cooking time. Ensure it's properly grilled.

In a bowl, add marmalade and lemon juice. Season with salt and pepper. Brush lamb chops with lemon and marmalade mix, cook for 2 minutes, turning once.

Cheesy Crab Appetizer

A delicious appetizer recipe with crab, cranberry sauce and cheese.

Makes: 6 servings

Prep: 5 min

Cook: 10 minutes

Ingredients:

- ½ cup lump crab meat
- 1/3 cup cream cheese, softened
- 15 phyllo mini shells, frozen
- ¼ cup canned cranberry sauce
- 2 tablespoons green onions, chopped
- Old bay seasoning to taste

Directions:

When ready to cook, whisk cranberry sauce in a bowl so that it smoothens. In a separate bowl, mix crab meat, old bay seasoning, green onion, and cream cheese. Gently fill each of the 15 shells with half teaspoon of cranberry sauce and half teaspoon of crab meat mixture. Place the shells in a frying pan and put on the low rack of your oven. Set temperature at 450F and cook for 10 minutes.

Halogen Lentil and Chicken

Delicious recipe with lentils and chicken.

Makes: 4 servings

Prep: 10 min

Cook: 40 min

Ingredients:

- 8 chicken thighs, skinless, boneless
- 1 cup green lentils, rinsed
- 3 tablespoon olive oil
- 1 cup chicken stock
- 2 garlic cloves, crushed
- 1 teaspoon coriander seeds
- 1 tablespoon light Muscovado sugar
- 2 red onions, thinly sliced
- 1 tsp cumin seed
- 2 tablespoons sun-dried tomato paste
- 1 can chopped tomatoes

Directions:

Grind a mixture of coriander seeds and cumin seeds using a mortar and pestle. Set aside. Add olive oil in a skillet and heat over medium. Rub chicken with salt and pepper and brown in hot oil, about 5 minutes. Stir often. Mix in onions, garlic, coriander, and cumin mixture. Remove from heat and transfer into a casserole dish.

In the same skillet, add chicken stock, tomato paste, sugar, and tomatoes. Bring the mixture to a boil. Add tomato mixture to chicken in the casserole dish. Mix in lentils and cover using foil. Put on the low rack of your halogen oven, set temperature at 400F, and let it cook for 40 min/until chicken is well cooked.

Roasted Apples

A delicious dessert that's easy and quick.

Makes: 1 serving

Prep: 10 min

Cook: 40 min

Ingredients:

- 1 apple, cored, peeled, chopped
- 3 ounces plain flour
- 2 ounces butter, melted
- 2 ounces brown sugar

Directions:

In a bowl, mix butter, brown sugar, & flour until well blended. In an oven safe dish, add apples and butter mixture. Toss gently and place on the high rack. Cook for 40 minutes at 350F.

Mint Lamb Chops

Delicious and tender lamb chops with just 5 ingredients!

Makes: 2 servings

Prep: 5 min

Cook: 10 min

Ingredients:

- 2 lamb chops
- 2 tablespoons mint, fresh
- Salt & freshly ground black pepper, to taste
- Freshly squeezed juice from half a lemon
- 2 tablespoons marmalade

Directions:

Preheat your oven to 400F.

Sprinkle lamb chops with salt & pepper and put on the high rack of your oven. Cook for 10 minutes, turning once during cooking time. Ensure it is properly grilled.

In a bowl, add marmalade and lemon juice. Season with salt and pepper. Brush lamb chops with lemon and marmalade mix, cook for 2 minutes, turning once.

Roasted Prawn

Roasted prawns with garlic and lemon juice.

Makes: 4 servings

Prep: 5 min

Cook: 10 min

Ingredients:

- 1.5 lb. prawns, peeled
- 2 garlic cloves, minced
- 2 teaspoons lemon juice, fresh
- ¼ cup margarine

Directions:

Preheat your oven to 420F.

In a small bowl, add garlic, margarine, and lemon juice. Mix to blend. Brush prawns with garlic mix. Put on the top rack of your oven. Grill prawns for 10 minutes, turning once during grilling.

Halogen Cod

A super easy and quick cod recipe with green pepper and mango chutney.

Makes: 2 servings

Prep: 5 min

Cook: 15 min

Ingredients:

- 2 cod fillets, skinless
- 1 tablespoons corn flour
- Tinned pineapple in juice
- 2 tablespoons tomato sauce
- 1 tablespoon vinegar
- 1 tablespoon olive oil
- ½ green pepper
- ½ onion, diced
- 1 tablespoon sugar
- 1 tablespoon mango chutney
- Salt and pepper to taste

Directions:

Rub cod fillets with olive oil and arrange on an oven tray. Season with salt and pepper, and place on the high rack of your oven. Set temperature at 400F and cook for 3 minutes. Turn and cook for another 3 minutes. Mix corn flour with little water in a bowl. Mix in pineapple, onion, tomato sauce, vinegar, green pepper, mango chutney, and sugar. Add pineapple mixture over cod and continue cooking for another 10 minutes.

Salmon and Asparagus

 A delicious and simple recipe with salmon, asparagus and sugar snap peas.

Makes: 4 servings

Prep: 10 min

Cook: 20 min

Ingredients:

- 6 stems of asparagus
- 4 salmon fillets
- 8 sugar snap peas, halved
- 4 tablespoon olive oil
- 1 tablespoon flat leaf parsley, chopped
- 2 garlic cloves
- 1 large shallot, peeled, sliced
- Salt and pepper to taste

Directions:

Prepare four pieces of foil. On each piece of foil, place one salmon fillet. On each fish fillet, add asparagus, snap peas, parsley, garlic cloves, shallot, salt and pepper. Sprinkle with olive oil. Carefully wrap the foil into a parcel. Arrange the parcels on the bottom of the rack of your oven. Now you can set temperature at 375F. Cook for 5 min/until the fish is well cooked.

Halogen Roast Salmon

Roasted salmon with pineapple and cinnamon.

Makes: 4 servings

Prep: 5 min

Cook: 8 min

Ingredients:

- 4 (6 ounces each) salmon fillets
- 4 slices pineapple rigs
- 2 teaspoons lemon zest
- 2 tablespoons fresh lemon juice
- ¼ teaspoon cinnamon
- 4 teaspoons chili powder
- ½ teaspoon salt
- 2 tablespoons brown sugar
- ¼ cup pineapple juice
- ¾ teaspoon ground cumin

Directions:

In a Ziploc bag, mix together lemon juice, pineapple juice, and salmon fillet. Seal and shake gently. Refrigerate for 1 hour. As it marinates, turn often. When ready to cook, mix lemon zest, sugar, cinnamon, salt, chili powder, and cumin in a small bowl. Remove fish from marinade and brush with chili mixture. Also brush pineapple slices with some of the chili mixture. Lightly coat the low rack of your oven with cooking spray. Set temperature at 450F. Put the pineapple slices and salmon fillets on the low rack of the oven. Grill for 5 min, turn, & continue grilling for another 3 to 4 minutes.

Halogen Asian Beef

Delicious Asian beef with soy sauce and ginger.

Makes: 6 servings

Prep: 10 min

Cook: 1 hr.

Ingredients:

- 1.5 lbs. lean braising steak, cut into small chunks
- 1 ½ cups sugar snap peas, halved
- ½ teaspoon red chili, dried
- 2 celery sticks
- 3 tablespoon wok oil
- ½ bunch spring onion
- 1 tablespoon dark soy sauce
- 1 tablespoon corn flour
- 14.5 fluid ounces hot beef stock
- 1 thumb size ginger, fresh, grated
- 2 tablespoons water
- 2 red peppers, cored, chopped

Directions:

Preheat your oven to 400F. Add 2 tbsp. of oil in a skillet and heat over medium. When hot, add meat, and cook until evenly browned. Place meat in a casserole dish.

In the same skillet, add reserved oil, and heat over medium. Mix in red pepper and celery. Cook until tender.

Add the mixture to beef in the casserole. Also add ginger, soy sauce, red chili, and beef stock. Mix well and cover using foil. Put on the low rack of your oven and cook for 50 minutes or until your meat is well cooked. In a bowl, mix together water & corn flour.

Mix into beef sauce. Add spring onions and peas. Cook covered for another 10 minutes.

Cheesy Italian Meat Loaf

Turkey meatloaf with sun-dried tomatoes and cheese.

Makes: 6 servings

Prep: 10 min

Cook: 35 min

Ingredients:

- 1 lb. turkey, ground
- 4 provolone cheese slices, stripped
- 2 large egg whites
- ½ cup tomatoes, sun-dried
- ¾ cup onion, chopped fine
- ¾ cup basil, fresh, chopped
- ½ cup ketchup
- 1 cup boiling water
- 1 cup breadcrumbs, seasoned
- 2 garlic cloves, minced
- 1 cup marinara sauce
- ½ cup provolone cheese, shredded

Directions:

In a bowl, add water and tomatoes. Let it soak for about 30 minutes. Remove tomatoes from water, drain, and chop. Set aside. In a large bowl, add turkey, egg whites, cheese, onion, garlic, basil, breadcrumbs, and ketchup.

Mix in chopped tomatoes. Mix well and make it into oval shaped loaves. Arrange the loaves on a baking pan. Set the temperature of your oven at 450F. Place the pan on the low rack and bake for 35 minutes. Serve topped with marinara and provolone strips.

Easy Beef Roast

An easy roast recipe with barbeque sauce.

Makes: 4 servings

Prep: 10 min

Cook: 15 min

Ingredients:

- 1 ½ lb. sirloin steak
- 1 teaspoon garlic salt
- 1 teaspoon celery salt
- 16 ounce barbeque sauce
- 1 tablespoon liquid smoke
- 1 teaspoon onion powder
- 2 tablespoons Worcestershire sauce

Directions:

Brush beef with celery salt, garlic salt, onion powder, Worcestershire sauce, and liquid smoke. Set your oven at 450F. Place the meat into the baking pan or frying pan and put on the high rack of your oven.

Cook for 10 minutes. Turn the meat and let it cook for another 2 minutes. Remove from the oven. Let it cool down and slice into thin slices. Sprinkle meat slices with barbeque sauce and cook in the oven for an additional 5 minutes.

Honey Mackerel

A quick and simple honey mackerel recipe.

Makes: 4 servings

Prep: 10 min

Cook: 20 min

Ingredients:

- 4 small whole mackerel, gutted, cleaned
- 2 tablespoons clear honey
- 2 teaspoons mint
- ½ cup apricot, chopped
- Salt and pepper to taste
- ¼ cup butter and extra for greasing
- ¼ cup Bulgur wheat
- 1 garlic clove, crushed
- 2 tablespoons double cream

Directions:

In a bowl, combine together honey, apricots, tarragon, garlic, wheat, mint, and salt and pepper. Spoon honey mixture into the cavities of the fish. Secure using a string and set aside. Prepare a shallow dish by brushing with butter. Arrange the fish in the dish. Add some butter. Use foil to cover the dish and put onto the low rack of your oven. Set temperature at 400F and cook for 20 minutes or until the meat is well cooked.

Conclusion

Well, there you go! 30 delicious recipes for you to try in your Halogen oven! Make sure you give each a recipe a go and don't forget to share them with your friends and family!

About the Author

Allie Allen developed her passion for the culinary arts at the tender age of five when she would help her mother cook for their large family of 8. Even back then, her family knew this would be more than a hobby for the young Allie and when she graduated from high school, she applied to cooking school in London. It had always been a dream of the young chef to study with some of Europe's best and she made it happen by attending the Chef Academy of London.

After graduation, Allie decided to bring her skills back to North America and open up her own restaurant. After 10 successful years as head chef and owner, she decided to sell her

Printed in Great Britain
by Amazon